The Magic Story

The Magic Story

by

Frederic Van Rensselaer Dey

As compiled by Cary M. West

The Magic Story

Written by Frederic Van Rensselaer Dey
and first published in 1903.

The original text is now in public domain.

ISBN-10: 1477590978
ISBN-13: 978-1477590973

Printed in the United States of America

Contents

Preface

"When the pupil is ready, the teacher appears."

Countless souls seek answers to the questions of life.

Our shelves and walls are lined with books. Computers, Ipads, and Kindles offer instant access via downloaded .pdf files. Self-help gurus flood the internet with their sure fire solutions to any problem you could ever imagine.

Yet lives remain difficult, and many struggle in their search for answers, their quest for the magic that will free them from their bondage.

Scores of unread books lay dormant gathering dust, their voices silenced by the demands of difficult lives. Trips to the local library or the corner bookstore give way to 99 cent downloads, which are then often "shelved" in favor of reading emails or surfing the web. Frustration leads to answers, yet in today's world there are so many self-help gurus, and so many thousands of websites, this information overload is often more confusing than its worth, and it's never free. The onslaught of newsletters, webinars, week long retreats, four week online courses, etc., is daunting, and they all have one thing in common. They want you to believe that you need them.

This is a quote from a website that publishes self-help books, "It's not about the books. It's really about reaching your target market and creating leads for products and services".

Sometimes it's simply a great pleasure to leave behind the good business sense, and subtle manipulation, and lose yourself in a magical story of discovery.

The Magic Story is one such pleasure. If you're not alone, and in an undisturbed quiet place, find that place now, because the Universe is about to speak to you.

In this timeless story from the early 1900's Sturtevant, a starving, struggling artist, sees his life change overnight after purchasing an old, ragged scrapbook for three pennies.

Inside this scrapbook is what he called "The Magic Story", because everyone he told it to prospered by it overnight like magic.

The benefit of this simple wisdom is freely given, as is everything in the Universe. How this wisdom is implemented rests solely within each individual.

Frederic Van Rensselaer Dey has outlined in this story a few simple lessons, his "recipe for success". Certainly, there is no reality where success is assured, and the method infallible, yet in his own words he says, "If followed, it can not fail. I place the burden of imparting to generations that are to come, the secret of this all-pervading good, the secret of being what you have it within you to be."

Sadly, Mr. Van Rensselaer Dey, a successful and prolific writer in his lifetime, found it necessary to take his own life at the age of 61.

A man of beautiful words, and goodness in his heart, he surely met with the minus-entity he wrote of.

Every life is a "Magic Story". Yours, mine. Look around you, they are everywhere. Look within, it is waiting.

Start tonight; start now upon this new journey.

***

While researching the origins of this book I have found two different versions. The first includes six lessons, and is the predominant version, both in print and on the internet. The second is comprised of ten lessons, and while I have not as yet been able to find a print version to validate this alternate ending, I have chosen to include it here, and leave the reader to decide its fate.

Find your quiet place. Sweep the dust from your heart.
Your task has just begun.

Cary M. West, 2012

Foreword

A Tribute To The Author
And The Story

***

The Magic Story written by Fredric Van Rensselaer Dey
in 1900, and published first in *Success Magazine,* was
later issued in book form by the publication, and ran in
many editions. It has been claimed for it that it contains
the philosophy of success. Whether this is so or not
depends upon the mental attitude and receptivity of
the reader. It is true that it has reclaimed men and
women from mistaken lives according to their personal
testimony. A clergyman from Cape Breton Island
wrote a letter to the author to say he would rather be
author of *The Magic Story* than the possessor of many
millions, adding "to be able to help mankind as this
story helps is to be blest indeed." There have been
thousands of similar testimonials.

Mr. Dey (1861-1922) was born in Watkins, N. Y. the son
of David P. and Emma Brewster Sayre Dey. On his
father's side he is descended from Dirck Jansen Dey,
who came from Amsterdam, Holland and settled in

New Amsterdam in 1641; on his mother's side he is descended from Thomas Sayre who was in Lynn, Mass. in 1638.

He attended the Columbia Law School and graduated in the class of 1883 and practiced law in Brooklyn for several years, was an assistant Corporation Counsel, a junior member of the law firm of William J. Gaynor, who later became the Mayor of New York.

Mr. Dey wrote under a score of pen names, notably "Nick Carter, Detective," of which he wrote more than a thousand stories.

When he wrote *The Magic Story*, I am sure that he had no idea that he had written a great story. He received fifty dollars for it, and it has been printed in various ways at least a million times. Corporations have found in it a stimulant to salesmanship and efficiency.

The Magic Story was an inspiration and was written in a period of great happiness.

... Haryot Holt Dey

One

The Magic Story

How *The Magic Story* was discovered...

Sturtevant's Story

I was sitting alone in the cafe and had just reached for the sugar preparatory to putting it into my coffee. Outside, the weather was hideous. Snow and sleet came swirling down, and the wind howled frightfully. Every time the outer door opened, a draft of unwelcome air penetrated the uttermost corners of the room. Still I was comfortable. The snow and sleet and wind conveyed nothing to me except an abstract thanksgiving that I was where it could not affect me. While I dreamed and sipped my coffee, the door opened and closed, and admitted - Sturtevant.

Sturtevant was an undeniable failure, but, withal, an artist of more than ordinary talent. He had, however, fallen into the rut traveled by ne'er-do-wells, and was out at the elbows as well as insolvent.

As I raised my eyes to Sturtevant's I was conscious of mild surprise at the change in his appearance. Yet he was not dressed differently. He wore the same threadbare coat in which he always appeared, and the old brown hat was the same. And yet there was something new and strange in his appearance. As he swished his hat around to relieve it of the burden of snow deposited by the howling nor'wester, there was something new in the gesticulation. I could not remember when I had invited Sturtevant to dine with me, but involuntarily I beckoned to him. He nodded and presently seated himself opposite to me. I asked him what he would have, and he, after scanning the bill of fare carelessly, ordered from it leisurely, and invited me to join him in coffee for two.

I watched him in stupid wonder, but, as I had invited the obligation, I was prepared to pay for it, although I knew I hadn't sufficient cash to settle the bill. Meanwhile I noticed the brightness of his usual lackluster eyes, and the healthful, hopeful glow upon his cheek, with increasing amazement.

"Have you lost a rich uncle?" I asked. "No," he replied, calmly, "but I have found my mascot." "Brindle, bull or terrier?" I inquired. "Currier," said Sturtevant, at length, pausing with his coffee cup half way to his lips, "I see that I have surprised you. It is not strange, for I am a surprise to myself. I am a new man, a different man, - and the alteration has taken place in the last few hours.

You have seen me come into this place 'broke' many a time, when you have turned away so that I would think you did not see me. I knew why you did that. It was not because you did not want to pay for a dinner, but because you did not have the money to do it. Is that your check? Let me have it. Thank you. I haven't any money with me tonight, but I, - well, this is my treat." He called the waiter to him, and, with an inimitable flourish, signed his name on the backs of the two checks, and waved him away. After that he was silent for a moment while he looked into my eyes, smiling at the astonishment which I in vain strove to conceal.

"Do you know an artist who possesses more talent than I?" he asked, presently. "No. Do you happen to know anything in the line of my profession that I could not accomplish, if I applied myself to it? No. You have been a reporter for the dailies for - how many? - seven or eight years. Do you remember when I ever had any credit until tonight? No. Was I refused just now? You have seen for yourself. Tomorrow my new career begins. Within a month I shall have a bank account. Why? Because I have discovered the secret of success."

"Yes," he continued, when I did not reply, "my fortune is made. I have been reading a strange story, and since reading it, I feel that my fortune is assured. It will make your fortune, too. All you have to do is read it. You have no idea what it will do for you. Nothing is impossible after you know that story. It makes everything as plain as A, B, C. The very instant you grasp its true meaning, success is certain. This morning I was a hopeless, aimless bit of garbage in the metropolitan ash can; tonight I wouldn't change places with a millionaire. That sounds foolish, but it is true. The millionaire has spent his enthusiasm; mine is all at hand."

11

"You amaze me," I said, wondering if he had been drinking absinthe.

"Won't you tell me the story? I should like to hear it."

"Certainly. I mean to tell it to the whole world. It is really remarkable that it should have been written and should remain in print so long, with never a soul to appreciate it until now. This morning I was starving. I hadn't any credit, nor a place to get a meal. I was seriously meditating suicide.

I had gone to three of the papers for which I had done work, and had been handed back all that I had submitted. I had to choose quickly between death by suicide and death slowly by starvation. Then I found the story and read it. You can hardly imagine the transformation. Why, my dear boy, everything changed at once, - and there you are."

"But what is the story, Sturtevant?"

"Wait; let me finish. I took those old drawings to other editors, and every one of them was accepted at once."
"Can the story do for others what it has done for you? For example, would it be of assistance to me?" I asked.
"Help you? Why not? Listen and I will tell it to you, although, really, you should read it. Still I will tell it as best I can. It is like this: you see, - - -"

The waiter interrupted us at that moment. He informed Sturtevant that he was wanted on the telephone, and with a word of apology, the artist left the table. Five minutes later I saw him rush out into the sleet and wind and disappear. Within the recollection

12

of the frequenters of that cafe, Sturtevant had never before been called out by telephone. That, of itself, was substantial proof of a change in his circumstances.

One night, on the street, I encountered Avery, a former college chum, then a reporter on one of the evening papers. It was about a month after my memorable interview with Sturtevant, which, by that time, was almost forgotten.

"Hello, old chap," he said; "how's the world using you? Still on space?"

"Yes," I replied, bitterly, "with prospects of being on the town, shortly. But you look as if things were coming your way. Tell me all about it.

"Things have been coming my way, for a fact, and it is all remarkable, when all is said. You know Sturtevant, don't you? It's all due to him. I was plumb down on my luck, - thinking of the morgue and all that, - looking for you, in fact, with the idea you would lend me enough to pay my room rent, when I met Sturtevant. He told me a story, and, really, old man, it is the most remarkable story you ever heard; it made a new man out of me. Within twenty-four hours I was on my feet and I've hardly known a care or a trouble since."

Avery's statement, uttered calmly, and with the air of one who had merely pronounced an axiom, recalled to my mind the conversation with Sturtevant in the cafe that stormy night, nearly a month before.
"It must be a remarkable story," I said, incredulously.
"Sturtevant mentioned it to me once. I have not seen him since. Where is he now?"

"He has been making war sketches in Cuba, at two hundred a week; he's just returned. It is a fact that everybody who has heard the story has done well since. There are Cosgrove and Phillips, - friends of mine, - you don't know them. One's a real estate agent; the other's a broker's clerk, Sturtevant told them the story, and they have experienced the same results that I have; and they are not the only ones.

"Do you know the story?" I asked. "Will you try its effect on me?"

"Certainly; with the greatest pleasure in the world. I would like to have it printed in big black type, and posted on the elevated stations throughout New York. It certainly would do a lot of good, and it's as simple as A, B, C: like living on a farm. Excuse me a minute, will you? I see Danforth over there. Back in a minute, old chap."

He nodded and smiled, - and was gone. I saw him join the man he had designated as Danforth. My attention was distracted for a moment, and when I looked up again, both had disappeared.

If the truth be told, I was hungry. My pocket at that moment contained exactly five cents; just enough to pay my fare up-town, but insufficient also to stand the expense of filling my stomach.

There was a "night owl" diner in the neighborhood, where I had frequently "stood up" the purveyor of midnight dainties, and to him I applied. He was

14

leaving the diner as I was on the point of entering it, and I accosted him.

"I'm broke again," I said, with extreme cordiality. "You'll have to trust me once more. Some ham and eggs, I think, will do for the present."

He coughed, hesitated a moment, and then re-entered the diner with me.

"Mr. Currier is good for anything he orders'" he said to the man in charge; "one of my old customers. This is Mr. Bryan, Mr. Currier. He will take good care of you, and 'stand for' you, just the same as I would. The fact is, I have sold out. I've just turned over the outfit to Bryan. By the way, isn't Mr. Sturtevant a friend of yours?" I nodded.

I couldn't have spoken if I had tried. "Well," continued the ex-"night owl" man, "he came in here one night, about a month ago, and told me the most wonderful story I ever heard. I've just bought a place in Eighth Avenue, where I am going to run a regular restaurant - near Twenty-third Street. Come and see me." He was out of the diner and the sliding door had been banged shut before I could stop him; so I ate my ham and eggs in silence, and resolved that I would hear that story before I slept. In fact, I began to regard it with superstition. If it had made so many fortunes, surely it should be capable of making mine.

The certainty that the wonderful story - I began to regard it as magic - was in the air, possessed me. As I started to walk homeward, fingering the solitary nickel in my pocket and contemplating the certainty of riding downtown in the morning, I experienced the sensation of something stealthily pursuing me, as if Fate were treading along behind me, yet never overtaking, and I was conscious that I was possessed with or by the story.

When I reached Union Square, I examined my address book for the home of Sturtevant. It was not recorded there. Then I remembered the cafe in University Place, and, although the hour was late, it occurred to me that he might be there. He was! In a far corner of the room, surrounded by a group of acquaintances, I saw him. He discovered me at the same instant, and motioned to me to join them at the table. There was no chance for the story, however. There were half a dozen around the table, and I was the furthest removed from Sturtevant. But I kept my eyes upon him, and bided my time, determined that, when he rose to depart, I would go with him.

A silence, suggestive of respectful awe, had fallen upon the party when I took my seat. Everyone had seemed to be thinking, and the attention of all was fixed upon Sturtevant. The cause was apparent. He had been telling the story. I had entered the cafe just too late to hear it. On my right, when I took my seat, was a doctor; on my left a lawyer. Facing me on the other side was a novelist with whom I had some acquaintance. The others were artists and newspaper men.

"It's too bad, Mr. Currier," remarked the doctor; "you should have come a little sooner, Sturtevant has been telling us a story; it is quite wonderful, really. I say, Sturtevant, won't you tell that story again, for the

16

benefit of Mr. Currier?" "Why yes. I believe that Currier has, somehow, failed to hear *The Magic Story*, although, as a matter of fact, I think he was the first one to whom I mentioned it at all. It was here, in this cafe, too, -at this very table.

Do you remember what a wild night that was, Currier? Wasn't I called to the telephone, or something like that? To be sure! I remember, now; interrupted just at the point when I was beginning the story. After that I told it to three or four fellows, and it 'braced them up,' as it had me. It seems incredible that a mere story can have such a tonic effect upon the success of so many persons who are engaged in such widely different occupations, but that is what it has done. It is a kind of never failing remedy, like a cough mixture that is warranted to cure everything, from a cold in the head to galloping consumption. There was Parsons, for example. He is a broker, you know, and had been on the wrong side of the market for a month. He had utterly lost his grip, and was on the verge of failure. I happened to meet him at the time he was feeling the bluest, and before we parted, something brought me around to the subject of the story, and I related it to him. It had the same effect on him as it had on me, and has had on everybody who has heard it, as far as I know.

I think you will all agree with me, that it is not the story itself that performs the surgical operation on the minds of those who are familiar with it; it is the way it is told, in print, I mean. The author has, somehow, produced a psychological effect which is indescribable. The reader is hypnotized. He receives a mental and moral tonic.

Perhaps, doctor, you can give some scientific explanation of the influence exerted by the story. It is a sort of elixir manufactured out of words, eh?" From that the company entered upon a general discussion of theories. Now and then slight references were made to the story itself, and they were just sufficient to tantalize me, -the only one present who had not heard it.

At length, I left my chair, and passing around the table, seized Sturtevant by one arm, and succeeded in drawing him away from the party.

"If you have any consideration for an old friend who is rapidly being driven mad by the existence of that confounded story, which Fate seems determined that I shall never hear, you will relate it to me now," I said, savagely. Sturtevant stared at me in wild surprise. "All right," he said. "The others will excuse me for a few moments, I think. Sit down here, and you shall have it. I found it pasted in an old scrapbook I purchased in Ann Street, for three cents and there isn't a thing about it by which one can get any idea in what publication it originally appeared, or who wrote it. When I discovered it, I began casually to read it, and in a moment I was interested. Before I left it, I had read it through many times, so that I could repeat it almost word for word. It affected me strangely, -as if I had come in contact with some strong personality.

There seems to be in the story a personal element that applies to every one who reads it. Well, after I had read it several times, I began to think it over. I couldn't stay in the house, so I seized my coat and hat and went out. I must have walked several miles, buoyantly, without realizing that I was the same man, who, in only a short

18

time before, had been in the depths of despondency. That was the day I met you here, -you remember."

We were interrupted at that instant by a uniformed messenger, who handed Sturtevant a telegram. It was from his chief, and demanded his instant attendance at the office. The sender had already been delayed an hour, and there was no help for it; he must go at once.

"Too bad!" said Sturtevant, rising and extending his hand. "Tell you what I'll do, old chap. I'm not likely to be gone any more than an hour or two. You take my key and wait for me in my room. In the escritoire near the window you will find an old scrapbook bound in rawhide. It was manufactured, I have no doubt, by the author of *The Magic Story*. Wait for me in my room until I return."

I found the book without difficulty. It was a quaint, home-made affair, covered, as Sturtevant had said, with rawhide, and bound with leather thongs. The pages formed an odd combination of yellow paper, vellum and homemade parchment. I found the story, curiously printed on the last-named material. It was quaint and strange. Evidently, the printer had "set" it under the supervision of the writer. The phraseology was an unusual combination of seventeenth and eighteenth century mannerisms, and the interpolation of italics and capitals could have originated in no other brain than that of its author. In reproducing the following story, the peculiarities of type, etc. are eliminated, but in other respects it remains unchanged.

Two

The Old Scrap Book

In as much as I have evolved from my experience the one great secret of success for all worldly undertakings, I deem it wise, now that the number of my days is nearly counted, to give to the generations that are to follow me the benefit of whatsoever knowledge I possess. I do not apologize for the manner of my expression, nor for the lack of literary merit, the latter being, I wot, its own apology. Tools much heavier than the pen have been my portion, and moreover, the weight of years has somewhat palsied the hand and brain; nevertheless, the fact I can tell, and what I deem the meat within the nut. What mattereth it, in what manner the shell be broken, so that the meat be obtained and rendered useful? I doubt not that I shall use, in the telling, expressions that have clung to my memory since childhood; for, when men attain the number of my years, happenings of youth are like to be clearer to their perceptions than are events of recent date; nor doth it matter much how a thought is expressed, if it be wholesome and helpful, and findeth the understanding.

Much have I wearied my brain anent the question, how best to describe this recipe for success that I have discovered, and it seemeth advisable to give it as it came to me; that is, if I relate somewhat of the story of my life, the directions for agglomerating the substances, and supplying the seasoning for the accomplishment of the dish, will plainly be perceived. Happen they may; and that men may be born generations after I am dust, who will live to bless me for the words I write.

My father, then, was a seafaring man who, early in life, forsook his vocation, and settled on a plantation in the colony of Virginia, where, some years thereafter, I was born, which event took place in the year 1642; and that was over a hundred years ago. Better for my father had it been, had he hearkened to the wise advice of my mother, that he remain in the calling of his education; but he would not have it so, and the good vessel he captained was bartered for the land I spoke of. Here beginneth the **first lesson** to be acquired:

Man should not be blinded to whatsoever merit exists in the opportunity which he hath in hand, remembering that a thousand promises for the future should weigh as naught against the possession of a single piece of silver.

When I had achieved ten years, my mother's soul took flight, and two years thereafter my worthy father followed her. I, being their only begotten, was left alone; howbeit, there were friends who, for a time, cared for me; that is to say, they offered me a home beneath their roof, - a thing which I took advantage of for the space of five months. From my father's estate there came to me naught; but, in the wisdom that came with increasing years, I convinced myself that his friend, under whose roof I lingered for some time, had defrauded him, and therefore me.

Of the time from the age of twelve and a half until I was three and twenty, I will make no recital here, since that time hath naught to do with this tale; but some time after, having in my possession the sum of sixteen guineas, ten, which I had saved from the fruits of my labor, I took ship to Boston town, where I began to work first as a cooper, and thereafter as a ship's carpenter, although always after the craft was docked; for the sea was not amongst my desires.

Fortune will sometimes smile upon an intended victim because of pure perversity of temper. Such was one of my experiences. I prospered, and at seven and twenty, owned the yard wherein, less than four years earlier, I had worked for hire. Fortune, howbeit, is a jade who must be coerced; she will not be coddled. Here beginneth the **second lesson** to be acquired:

Fortune is ever elusive, and can only be retained by force. Deal with her tenderly and she will forsake you for a stronger man. (In that, me- thinks, she is not unlike other women of my knowledge.)

About this time, Disaster (which is one of the heralds of broken spirits and lost resolve), paid me a visit. Fire ravaged my yards, leaving me nothing in its blackened paths but debts, which I had not the coin wherewith to defray. I labored with my acquaintances, seeking assistance for a new start, but the fire that had burned my competence, seemed also to have consumed their sympathies. So it happened, within a short time, that not only had I lost all, but I was hopelessly indebted to others; and for that they cast me into prison. It is possible that I might have rallied from my losses but for this last indignity, which broke down my spirits so that I became utterly despondent. Upward of a year I was detained within the gaol; and, when I did come forth, it was not the same hopeful, happy man, content with his lot, and with confidence in the world and its people, who had entered there.

Life has many pathways, and of them by far the greater number lead downward. Some are precipitous, others are less abrupt; but ultimately, no matter at what inclination the angle may be fixed, they arrive at the same destination, - failure. And here beginneth the **third lesson:**

Failure exists only in the grave. Man, being alive, hath not yet failed; always he may turn about and ascend by the same path he descended by; and there may be one that is less abrupt (albeit longer of achievement), and more adaptable to his condition.

When I came forth from prison, I was penniless. In all the world I possessed naught beyond the poor garments which covered me, and a walking stick which the turnkey had permitted me to retain, since it was worthless. Being a skilled workman, howbeit, I speedily found employment at good wages; but, having eaten of the fruit of worldly advantage, dissatisfaction possessed me. I became morose and sullen; whereat, to cheer my spirits, and for the sake of forgetting the losses I had sustained, I passed my evenings at the tavern. Not that I drank overmuch of

24

liquor, except on occasion (for I have ever been somewhat abstemious), but that I could laugh and sing, and parry wit and *badinage* with my ne'er-do-well companions; and here might be included the **fourth lesson:**

Seek comrades among the industrious, for those who are idle will sap your energies from you.

It was my pleasure at that time to relate, upon slight provocation, the tale of my disasters, and to rail against the men whom I deemed to have wronged me, because they had seen fit not to come to my aid. Moreover, I found childish delight in filching from my employer, each day, a few moments of the time for which he paid me. Such a thing is less honest than downright theft.

This habit continued and grew upon me until the day dawned which found me not only without employment, but also without character, which meant that I could not hope to find work with any other employer in Boston town.

It was then that I regarded myself a failure. I can liken my condition at that time for naught more similar than that of a man who, descending the steep side of a mountain loses his foothold. The farther he slides, the faster he goes. I have also heard this condition described by the word Ishmaelite, which I understand to be a man whose hand is against everybody, and who thinks that the hands of every other man are against him; and here beginneth the **fifth lesson:**

The Ishmaelite and the leper are the same, since both are abominations in the sight of man - albeit they differ much, in that the former may be restored to perfect health. The former is entirely the result of imagination; the latter has poison in his blood.

I will not discourse at length upon the gradual degeneration of my energies. It is not meet ever to dwell much upon misfortunes (which saying is also worthy of remembrance).

It is enough if I add that the day came where I possessed naught wherewith to purchase food and raiment, and I found myself like unto a pauper, save at infrequent times when I could earn a few pence, or mayhap, a shilling. Steady employment I could not secure, so I became emaciated in body, and naught but skeleton in spirit.

***

* Here is where the two versions go their separate ways. There is no right or wrong in the Universe, there just is. Such is the case here. * Publisher's note. *

***

My condition, then, was deplorable; not so much for the body, be it said, as for the mental part of me, which was sick unto death. In my imagination I deemed myself ostracized by the whole world, for I had sunk very low indeed; and here beginneth the **sixth and final lesson** to be acquired, (which cannot be told in

26

one sentence, nor in one paragraph, but must needs be adopted from the remainder of this tale).

Well do I remember my awakening, for it came in the night, when, in truth, I did awake from sleep. My bed was a pile of shavings in the rear of the cooper shop where once I had worked for hire; my roof was the pyramid of casks, underneath which I had established myself. The night was cold, and I was chilled, albeit, paradoxically, I had been dreaming of light and warmth and of the depletion of good things. You will say, when I relate the effect the vision had on me, that my mind was affected. So be it, for it is the hope that the minds of others might be likewise influenced which disposes me to undertake the labor of this writing. It was the dream which converted me to the belief - nay, to the knowledge - that I was possessed of two entities: and it was my own better self that afforded me the assistance for which I had pleaded in vain from my acquaintances. I have heard this condition described by the word "double." Nevertheless, that word does not comprehend my meaning. A double, can be naught more than a double, neither half being possessed of individuality. But I will not philosophize, since philosophy is naught but a suit of garments for the decoration of a dummy figure.

Moreover, it was not the dream itself which affected me; it was the impression made by it, and the influence that it exerted over me, which accomplished my enfranchisement. In a word, then, I encouraged my other identity. After toiling through a tempest of snow and wind, I peered into a window and saw that other being. He was rosy with health; before him, on the hearth, blazed a fire of logs; there was a conscious power and force in his demeanor; he was phisically and mentally muscular. I rapped timidly upon the door, and he bade me enter. There was a not unkindly smile of derision in his eyes as he motioned me to a chair by the fire; but he uttered no word of welcome; and, when I had warmed myself, I went forth again into the tempest, burdened with the shame which the contrast between us had forced upon me. It was then that I awoke; and here cometh the strange part of my tale, for, when I did awake, I was not alone. There was a Presence with me; intangible to others, I discovered later, but real to me.

The Presence was in my likeness, yet it was strikingly unlike. The brow, not more lofty than my own, yet seemed more round and full; the eyes, clear, direct, and filled with purpose, glowed with enthusiasm and resolution; the lips, chin - ay, the whole contour of face and figure was dominant and determined. He was calm, steadfast, and self-reliant; I was cowering, filled with nervous trembling, and fearsome of intangible shadows. When the Presence turned away, I followed, and throughout the day I never lost sight of it, save when it disappeared for a time beyond some doorway where I dared not enter; at such places, I awaited its return with trepidation and awe, for I could not help wondering at the temerity of the Presence (so like myself, and yet so unlike) in daring to enter where my own feet feared to tread.

It seemed also as if purposely, I was led to the place and to the men where, and before whom I most dreaded to appear; to offices where once I had transacted business; to men with whom I had financial dealings. Throughout the day I pursued the Presence, and at evening saw it disappear beyond the portals of a hostelry famous for its cheer and good living. I sought the pyramid of casks and shavings.

Not again in my dreams that night did I encounter the Better Self (for that is what I have named it), albeit, when, perchance, I awakened from slumber, it was near to me, ever wearing that calm smile of kindly derision which could not be mistaken for pity, nor for condolence in any form. The contempt of it stung me sorely.

The second day was not unlike the first, being a repetition of its forerunner, and I was again doomed to wait outside during the visits which the Presence paid to places where I fain would have gone had I possessed the requisite courage. It is fear which deporteth a man's soul from his body and rendereth it a thing to be despised. Many a time I essayed to address it but enunciation rattled in my throat, unintelligible; and the day closed like its predecessor. This happened many days, one following another, until I ceased to count them; albeit, I discovered that constant association with the Presence was producing an effect on me; and one night when I awoke among the casks and discerned that he was present, I made bold to speak, albeit with marked timidity.

"Who are you?" I ventured to ask; and I was startled into an upright posture by the sound of my own voice; and the question seemed to give pleasure to my companion, so that I fancied there was less of derision in his smile when he responded.

"I am that I am," was the reply. "I am he who you have been; I am he who you may be again; wherefore do you hesitate? I am he who you were, and whom you have cast out for other company. I am the man made in the image of God, who once possessed your body. Once we dwelt within it together, not in harmony, for that can never be, nor yet in unity, for that is impossible, but as tenants in common who rarely fought for full possession. Then, you were a puny thing, but you became selfish and exacting until I could no longer abide with you, therefore I stepped out. There is a plus-entity and minus-entity in every human body that is born into the world. Whichever one of these is favored by the flesh becomes dominant; then is the other inclined to abandon its habitation, temporarily or for all time. I am the plus-entity of yourself; you are the minus-entity. I own all things; you possess naught. That body which we both inhabited is mine, but it is unclean, and I will not dwell within it. Cleanse it, and I will take possession."

"Why do you pursue me?" I next asked of the Presence.

"You have pursued me, not I you. You can exist without me for a time, but your path leads downward, and the end is death. Now that you approach the end, you debate if it be not politic that you should cleanse your house and invite me to enter. Step aside, from the brain and the will; cleanse them of your presence; only on that condition will I ever occupy them again."

"The brain has lost its power," I faltered. "The will is a weak thing, now; can you repair them?"

"**Listen!**" said the Presence, and he towered over me while I cowered abjectly at his feet.

"To the plus-entity of a man, all things are possible. The world belongs to him, - is his estate. He fears naught, dreads naught, stops at naught; he asks no privileges, but demands them; he dominates, and cannot cringe; his requests are orders; opposition flees at his approach; he levels mountains, fills in vales, and travels on an even plane where stumbling is unknown."

Thereafter, I slept again, and, when I awoke, I seemed to be in a different world. The sun was shining and I was conscious that birds twittered above my head. My body, yesterday trembling and uncertain, had become vigorous and filled with energy. I gazed upon the pyramid of casks in amazement that I had so long made use of it for an abiding place, and I was wonderingly conscious that I had passed my last night beneath its shelter.

The events of the night recurred to me, and I looked about me for the Presence. It was not visible, but anon I discovered, cowering in a far corner of my resting place, a puny abject shuddering figure, distorted of visage, deformed of shape, disheveled and unkempt of appearance. It tottered as it walked, for it approached me piteously; but I laughed aloud, mercilessly. Perchance I knew then that it was the minus-entity, and that the plus-entity was within me; albeit I did not then realize it. Moreover, I was in haste to get away; I had no time for philosophy. There was much for me to do - much; strange it was that I had not thought of that yesterday. But yesterday was gone - today was with me - it had just begun.

As had once been my daily habit, I turned my steps in the direction of the tavern, where formerly I had partaken of my meals. I nodded cheerily as I entered, and smiled in recognition of returned salutations. Men who had ignored me for months bowed graciously when I passed them on the thoroughfare. I went to the washroom, and from there to the breakfast table; afterwards, when I passed the taproom, I paused a moment and said to the landlord:

"I will occupy the same room that I formerly used, if perchance, you have it at disposal. If not, another will do as well, until I can obtain it."

Then I went out and hurried with all haste to the cooperage. There was a huge wain in the yard, and men were loading it with casks for shipment. I asked no questions, but, seizing barrels, began hurling them to the men who worked atop of the load. When this was finished, I entered the shop. There was a vacant bench; I recognized its disuse by the litter on its top. It was the same at which I had once worked. Stripping off my coat, I soon cleared it of impedimenta. In a moment more I was seated, with my foot on the vice-lever, shaving staves.

It was an hour later when the master workman entered the room, and he paused in surprise at sight of me; already there was a goodly pile of neatly shaven staves beside me, for in those days I was an excellent workman; there was none better, but, alas! now, age hath deprived me of my skill. I replied to his unasked question with the brief, but comprehensive sentence: "I have returned to work, sir." He nodded his head and passed on, viewing the work of other men, albeit anon he glanced askance in my direction. Here endeth the sixth and last lesson to be acquired, although there is more to be said, since from that moment I was a successful man, and ere long possessed another shipyard, and had acquired a full competence of worldly goods.

I pray you who read, heed well the following admonitions, since upon them depend the word "success" and all that it implies:

Whatsoever you desire of good is yours. You have but to stretch forth your hand and take it.

Learn that the consciousness of dominant power within you is the possession of all things attainable.

Have no fear of any sort or shape, for fear is an adjunct of the minus-entity. If you have skill, apply it; the world must profit by it, and therefore, you.

Make a daily and nightly companion of your plus-entity; if you heed its advice, you cannot go wrong.

Remember, philosophy is an argument; the world, which is your property, is an accumulation of facts.

Go therefore, and do that which is within you to do; take no heed of gestures which would beckon you aside; **ask of no man permission to perform.**

The minus-entity requests favors; the plus-entity grants them. Fortune waits upon every footstep you take; seize her, bind her, hold her, for she is yours; she belongs to you.

Start out now, with these admonitions in your mind.

Stretch out your hand, and grasp the plus, which, maybe, you have never made use of, save in great emergencies. Life is an emergency most grave. Your plus-entity is beside you now; cleanse your brain, and strengthen your will. It will take possession. It waits upon you.

Start tonight; start now upon this new journey.

Be always on your guard. Whichever entity controls you, the other hovers at your side; beware lest the evil enter, even for a moment.

My task is done. I have written the recipe for "success." If followed, it cannot fail.

Wherein I may not be entirely comprehended, the plus-entity of whosoever reads will supply the deficiency; and upon that Better Self of mine, I place the burden of imparting to generations that are to come, the secret of this all-pervading good - the secret of being what you have it within you to be.

***

The End

A Different Drummer

My condition, then, was deplorable; not so much for the body, be it said, as for the mental part of me, which was sick unto death. In my imagination I deemed myself ostracized by the whole world, for I had sunk very low indeed; and here beginneth the **sixth lesson** to be acquired:

Poverty is very agonizing, and in some men it kills the
very soul but it is the icy North wind
that lashes men into Vikings. Poverty is terrorful,
I must aver, but in many cases,
the best thing that can happen to a young man
is to be tossed overboard and be compelled
to sink or swim for himself.

He is not acquainted with himself nor with others who hath not known adversity. Continual success shows us but one side of the world. Success surrounds us with friends who only praise and flatter us and is only in failure that we hear from our enemies who extol not our virtues but from whom alone we can learn our defects.

35

Truly Providence works in strange ways, my brethren, and until a man comes to the autumn of his days, he can scarce say what hath been ill-luck and what hath been good. For of all the seeming misfortunes which have befallen me during my life, there is not one which I have not come to look upon as a blessing. And if you once take this into your hearts, it is a mighty help in enabling you to meet all troubles with a stiff lip; for why should a man grieve when he hath not yet determined whether what hath chanced may not prove to be a cause of rejoicing?

For my own part, believing as I now do that there is nothing of chance in this world. I feel that I had been exposed to these trials in order to dispose me toward finding my real Ego Self and that I had been saved in order to put this finding into effect. As an earnest of my endeavor to do so, I oft times kneel down and pray that I may be of some use on the earth and that I might be helped to rise above my own wants and interests, to aid forward whatever of good or noble might be stirring in my days. It is well nigh seventy years since I have found The Presence, but I can truly say that from that day to this the aims which I have laid down for myself have served me as a compass over the dark waters of life – a compass which I may perchance not always follow, for flesh is weak and frail, but which hath, at least, been ever present, that I might turn to it in seasons of doubt and of danger.

Well do I remember my awakening, for it came in the night, when, in truth, I did awake from sleep. My bed was a pile of shavings in the rear of the cooper shop where once I had worked for hire; my roof was the pyramid of casks, underneath which I had established myself. The night was cold, and I was chilled, albeit, paradoxically, I had been dreaming of light and warmth and of the depletion of good things. You will say, when I relate the effect the vision had on me, that my mind was affected. So be it, for it is the hope that the minds of others might be likewise influenced which disposes me to undertake the labor of this writing. It was the dream which converted me to the belief - nay, to the knowledge - that I was possessed of two entities: and it was my own better self that afforded me the assistance for which I had pleaded in vain from my acquaintances. I have heard this condition described by the word "double." Nevertheless, that word does not comprehend my meaning. A double, can be naught more than a double, neither half being possessed of individuality. But I will not philosophize, since philosophy is naught but a suit of garments for the decoration of a dummy figure.

Moreover, it was not the dream itself which affected me; it was the impression made by it, and the influence that it exerted over me, which accomplished my enfranchisement. In a word, then, I encouraged my other identity. After toiling through a tempest of snow and wind, I peered into a window and saw that other being. He was rosy with health; before him, on the hearth, blazed a fire of logs; there was a conscious power and force in his demeanor; he was physically and mentally muscular. I rapped timidly upon the door, and he bade me enter. There was a not unkindly smile of derision in his eyes as he motioned me to a chair by the fire; but he uttered no word of welcome; and, when I had warmed myself, I went forth again into the tempest, burdened with the shame which the contrast between us had forced upon me. It was then that I awoke; and here cometh the strange part of my tale, for, when I did awake, I was not alone. There was a Presence with me; intangible to others, I discovered later, but real to me.

The Presence was in my likeness, yet it was strikingly unlike. The brow, not more lofty than my own, yet seemed more round and full; the eyes, clear, direct, and filled with purpose, glowed with enthusiasm and resolution; the lips, chin, - ay, the whole contour of face and figure was dominant and determined.

He was calm, steadfast, and self-reliant; I was cowering, filled with nervous trembling, and fearsome of intangible shadows. When the Presence turned away, I followed, and throughout the day I never lost sight of it, save when it disappeared for a time beyond some doorway where I dared not enter; at such places, I awaited its return with trepidation and awe, for I could not help wondering at the temerity of the Presence (so like myself, and yet so unlike), in daring to enter where my own feet feared to tread.

It seemed also as if purposely, I was led to the place and to the men where, and before whom I most dreaded to appear; to offices where once I had transacted business; to men with whom I had financial dealings. Throughout the day I pursued the Presence, and at evening saw it disappear beyond the portals of a hostelry famous for its cheer and good living. I sought the pyramid of casks and shavings.

Not again in my dreams that night did I encounter the Better Self (for that is what I have named it), albeit, when, perchance, I awakened from slumber, it was

38

near to me, ever wearing that calm smile of kindly derision which could not be mistaken for pity, nor for condolence in any form. The contempt of it stung me sorely.

The second day was not unlike the first, being a repetition of its forerunner, and I was again doomed to wait outside during the visits which the Presence paid to places where I fain would have gone had I possessed the requisite courage. It is fear which deporteth a man's soul from his body and rendereth it a thing to be despised. Many a time I essayed to address it but enunciation rattled in my throat, unintelligible; and the day closed like its predecessor.

This happened many days, one following another, until I ceased to count them; albeit, I discovered that constant association with the Presence was producing an effect on me; and one night when I awoke among the casks and discerned that he was present, I made bold to speak, albeit with marked timidity.

"Who are you?" I ventured to ask; and I was startled into an upright posture by the sound of my own voice; and the question seemed to give pleasure to my companion, so that I fancied there was less of derision in his smile when he responded.

"I am that I am," was the reply. "I am he who you have been; I am he who you may be again; wherefore do you hesitate? I am he who you were, and whom you have cast out for other company. I am the man made in the image of God, who once possessed your body. Once we dwelt within it together, not in harmony, for that can never be, nor yet in unity, for that is impossible, but as tenants in common who rarely fought for full possession. Then, you were a puny thing, but you became selfish and exacting until I could no longer abide with you, therefore I stepped out. There is a plus-entity and minus-entity in every human body that is born into the world. Whichever one of these is favored by the flesh becomes dominant; then is the other inclined to abandon its habitation, temporarily or for all time. I am the plusentity of yourself; you are the minus-entity. I own all things; you possess naught. That body which we both inhabited is mine, but it is unclean, and I will not dwell within it. Cleanse it, and I will take possession."

"Why do you pursue me?" I next asked of the Presence.

"You have pursued me, not I you. You can exist without me for a time, but your path leads downward, and the end is death. Now that you approach the end, you debate if it be not politic that you should cleanse your house and invite me to enter. Step aside, from the brain and the will; cleanse them of your presence; only on that condition will I ever occupy them again."

"The brain has lost its power," I faltered. "The will is a weak thing, now; can you repair them?"

"*Listen!*" said the Presence, and he towered over me while I cowered abjectly at his feet. "To the plus-entity of a man, all things are possible. The world belongs to him, - is his estate. He fears naught, dreads naught, stops at naught; he asks no privileges, but demands them; he dominates, and cannot cringe; his requests are orders; opposition flees at his approach; he levels

40

mountains, fills in vales, and travels on an even plane where stumbling is unknown."

Thereafter, I slept again, and, when I awoke, I seemed to be in a different world. The sun was shining and I was conscious that birds twittered above my head. My body, yesterday trembling and uncertain, had become vigorous and filled with energy. I gazed upon the pyramid of casks in amazement that I had so long made use of it for an abiding place, and I was wonderingly conscious that I had passed my last night beneath its shelter.

The events of the night recurred to me, and I looked about me for the Presence. It was not visible, but anon I discovered, cowering in a far corner of my resting place, a puny abject shuddering figure, distorted of visage, deformed of shape, disheveled and unkept of appearance. It tottered as it walked, for it approached me piteously; but I laughed aloud, mercilessly. Perchance I knew then that it was the minus-entity, and that the plus-entity was within me; albeit I did not then realize it. Moreover, I was in haste to get away; I had no time for philosophy. There was much for me to do, - much; strange it was that I had not thought of that yesterday. But yesterday was gone, - today was with me, - it had just begun.

As had once been my daily habit, I turned my steps in the direction of the tavern, where formerly I had partaken of my meals. I nodded cheerily as I entered, and smiled in recognition of returned salutations. Men who had ignored me for months bowed graciously when I passed them on the thoroughfare. I went to the washroom, and from there to the breakfast table;

afterwards, when I passed the taproom, I paused a moment and said to the landlord:

"I will occupy the same room that I formerly used, if perchance, you have it at disposal. If not, another will do as well, until I can obtain it."

Then I went out and hurried with all haste to the cooperage. There was a huge wain in the yard, and men were loading it with casks for shipment. I asked no questions, but, seizing barrels began hurling them to the men who worked atop of the load. When this was finished, I entered the shop. There was a vacant bench; I recognized its disuse by the litter on its top. It was the same at which I had once worked. Stripping off my coat, I soon cleared it of impedimenta. In a moment more I was seated, with my foot on the vice-lever, shaving staves.

It was an hour later when the master workman entered the room, and he paused in surprise at sight of me; already there was a goodly pile of neatly shaven staves beside me, for in those days I was an excellent workman; there was none better, but, alas! now, age hath deprived me of my skill. I replied to his unasked question with the brief, but comprehensive sentence: "I have returned to work, sir." He nodded his head and passed on, viewing the work of other men, albeit anon he glanced askance in my direction.

From that moment I was a successful man and ere long possessed another shipyard, and had acquired a full competence of worldly goods.

Here ensues the **seventh lesson** for the emolument of your inquiry after truth:

God placed you here for the purpose of
seeking Self Mastery and Virtue.

The presence of a table doth prove the existence of a carpenter and so the presence of a universe proves the existence of a universe maker, call Him by what name you will. So far the ground is very firm beneath us, without either inspiration, teaching. or any aid whatever. Since then, there *must* be a world-maker, let us judge of His nature by His work. We cannot observe the glories of the firmament, its infinite extent, its beauty, and the divine skill wherewith every plant and animal hath its wants cared for, without seeing that He is full of wisdom, intelligence and power. We are still, you will perceive, upon solid ground, without having to call to our aid aught save pure reason.

Having got so far, let us inquire to what end the universe was made and we put upon it. The teaching of all nature shows that it must be to the end of improvement and upward growth, the increase in real virtue, in knowledge and in wisdom. Nature is a silent preacher which holds forth upon week-days as on Sabbaths. We see the acorn grow into the oak tree, the egg into the bird, the maggot into the butterfly. Shall we doubt then, that the human soul, the most precious of all things, is also upon the upward path? And how can the soul progress save through the cultivation of virtue and self-mastery? What other way is there? There is none. We may say with confidence, then that we are placed here to increase in knowledge and virtue.

This is the core of all religion, and this much needs not faith in the acceptance. It is as true and as capable of proof as one of the exercises of Euclid. On this common ground men have raised many different buildings. Christianity, the creed of Mohammed, the creed of the Easterners, have all the same essence. The difference lies in forms and details. Let us hold to our own Christian creed, the beautiful often professed and seldom-practiced doctrine of love, but let us not despise our fellowmen, for we are all branches from the common root of truth.

Man comes out of darkness into light. He tarries a while and then passes into darkness again. Brethren, the days are passing. Let them not be wasted. They are few in number. What says Petrarch? "To him that enters, life seems infinite to him that departs, nothing." Let every day, every hour, be spent in furthering the Creator's end – in getting out whatever power for good there is in you. What is pain, or work or trouble? The cloud that passes over the sun. But the result of work well done is everything. It is eternal. It lives and waxes stronger through the centuries. Pause not for a rest. The rest will come when the hour of work is past. May God protect and guide you. The **eighth lesson** for your inculcation;

Your daily life drama is not unlike
the dream state at night.

As the dreamer of night dreams, perceiving that he is dreaming, may fashion the dream to his fancy; may build a stately palace; court a beautiful damsel; fly through the air; have the dream as he pleases. So verily, with the understanding that you are your Ego-Self, you may go forth in this world and have things come to pass as you decree. Your word is the law to your own circumstances. Then only, will you awaken from your nightmare of mortal existence and find yourself in the world of sunlight and pure peace. You can never be held in bondage to the lies of the senses after you see their nothingness. None of these phantasies of a dream world drama can harm you for there is no reality in them.

Look not backwards in memory and grieve because of false steps you have taken, labors lost, and precious years wasted. This is a dream you are awakened from. Turn your mind to the glorious future that awaits you as a Son of God. Cast behind you forever the grotesque imaginings of the dream of lack and misfortune, of slavery and bondage, of fear thought and dread, and step forward in the glorious spirit of Positive existence facing the world as a Master. You must make your own choice – no one else may make it for you. Thus will dawn the Age of the Superman; that godlike Man in whom will be vested the inheritances of the earth. The **ninth guidepost** for your disclosure;

Hold the ship of your life steadfast on
the course you have set for yourself.
Heed not those who would dissuade,
discomfit, or detain you.

Your minus-entity will ever make contentions with you as to the hopelessness of your aims and purposes, and goals. It will bring temptation to you to show others your charts, course and destination; to lessen your work; to loose faith in the Power of your Silent Partner. It will stop at nothing in its attempt to discourage you from the work you have set for yourself. Stand firmly on your own two feet as pilot of your ship and hold the helm steadfast to the course of your voyage over the seas of life. Declare, "Minus-entity, Obey; I am the Master here."

Are you to acknowledge obstacles or enemies? Not so. When you take cognizance of them, you admit that they have power to oppress or disturb you. This they have not, for your Super Ego has all power and therefore cannot be obstructed or shackled by anything less contriving to do so. In admittance of their abilities to stop you, you enhance them with strength they possess not in sooth; else how may a lesser restrain a higher power? This cannot be. Oftimes as your minus-entity succumbs to emotions of hate, jealousy, criticism, envy, you weaken your own state and help those to whom your thoughts are directed. You have given them some of your vitality through thoughts, and weakened yourself in the measure.

What is to be then your frame of mind? How feels the wind if it could discourse with it yourself on the subject? It blows as it listeth and no man or thing, may stop it. They that revile and persecute you are you helping you, in sooth, through all unknowing to themselves. Through them alone, you may be goaded on to greater accomplishments. Does not the bird fly because of the air that doth resist its wings? So does this lesson bear application to you?

Lesson Ten: Victorious Living and Success through partnership with the Presence:

I pray you who read, heed well the following admonitions, since upon them depend the word "success" and all that it implies:

> *Whatsoever you desire of good is yours. You have but to stretch forth your hand and take it. Learn that the consciousness of dominant power within you is the possession of all things attainable.*

Have no fear of any sort or shape, for fear is an adjunct of the minus-entity.

If you have skill, apply it; the world must profit by it, and therefore, you.

Make a daily and nightly companion of your plus-entity; if you heed its advice, you cannot go wrong.

Remember, philosophy is an argument; the world, which is your property, is an accumulation of facts.

Go therefore, and do that which is within you to do; take no heed of gestures which would beckon you aside; *ask of no man permission to perform.*

The minus-entity requests favors; the plus-entity grants them. Fortune waits upon every footstep you take; seize her, bind her, hold her, for she is yours; she belongs to you.

Start out now, with these admonitions in your mind.

Stretch out your hand, and grasp the plus, which, maybe, you have never made use of, save in great emergencies. Life is an emergency most grave.

Your plus-entity is beside you now; cleanse your brain, and strengthen your will. It will take possession. It waits upon you.

Start tonight; start now upon this new journey.

Be always on your guard. Whichever entity controls you, the other hovers at your side; beware lest the evil enter, even for a moment.

My task is done. I have written the recipe for "success." If followed, it cannot fail.

Wherein I may not be entirely comprehended, the plus-entity of whosoever reads will supply the deficiency; and upon that Better Self of mine, I place the burden of imparting to generations that are to come, the secret of this all-pervading good, -the secret of being what you have it within you to be.

***

"There are no times in life when opportunities, the chance to be and do, gather so richly about the soul as when it has to suffer. Then everything depends on whether the man turns to the lower or the higher helps. If he resorts to mere expedients and tricks, the opportunity is lost. He comes out no richer, nor greater; nay, he comes out harder, poorer, smaller for his pain. But, if he turns to God, the hour of suffering is the turning of his life." ... Phillips Brooks.

***

**Start tonight; start now upon this new journey.**

The goal of Fathomless Sea Publishing is to fuel the dreams of readers, researchers, and teachers by offering timeless, and often hard to find, original publications for print.

Maintaining the integrity of these original works is fundamental to the form in which we create new editions, and every effort is made to work competently within the constraints of digitized scans and public domain websites. In this age of eBooks and eReaders we believe that there are still among us those that enjoy turning the pages of a good book. While we embrace technology, we also cherish tradition.

In providing you with quality products we choose to add minimal editorial content, reserving the rights of readers to develop their own interpretations, and very simply, hope that we do our part in the preservation of historic literature.

While preserving and promoting the legacy of literary history is the spirit in which we offer these new editions, equitable prices for publication, time, and materials must necessarily be set to cover incurred costs. Because Open Source projects are the main source of our material, we strive to give back by supporting various projects with a portion of our profits. Given the nature of the world's historic literature, furthering the mutual goal of sharing timeless words with a larger audience will always have a happy ending.

We thank you sincerely for your patronage and support.

Fathomless Sea Publishing

fseapub.com

50

Printed in Great Britain
by Amazon